God's Plan For Ishmael

ישמעאל

Mrs. Cheryl Zehr

I0162263

Olive Press
צהר זית

Messianic & Christian Publisher

www.olivepresspublisher.org

Published by
Olive Press צהר זית
Messianic and Christian Publisher
P.O. Box 567
Port Leyden, NY 13433
    and
1326 N. Winton Rd.
Rochester, NY 14609

Our prayer at Olive Press is that we may help make the Word of Adonai fully known, that it spread rapidly and be glorified everywhere. We hope our books help open people's eyes so they will turn from darkness to Light and from the power of the adversary to God and to trust in ישוע Yeshua (Jesus). (From II Thess. 3:1; Col. 1:25; Acts 26:18,15 NRSV and CJB, the *Complete Jewish Bible*) May this book in particular inspire people to intercede for those trapped in Islam.

www.olivepresspublisher.org

Cover and interior design by the author.
Cover photos and photo on p. 62 by the author on her world travels.
Photo on p. 57 is from http://hitch.south.cx/pictures.htm
Other photos and graphics are from Microsoft Office Online Clipart

Printed in the USA
ISBN 978-0-9790873-6-3
Christian Life: 1. Political Issues 2. Prayer 3. Spiritual Warfare

God's Plan for Ishmael ישמעאל

All scriptures, unless otherwise indicated, are taken from the *New Revised Standard Version* (NRSV) of the Bible, copyright © 1989 National Council of the Churches of Christ in the USA. All rights reserved.

Scriptures marked CJB are taken from the *Complete Jewish Bible*. Copyright © 1998 by David H. Stern. All rights reserved.

In honor to God, all pronouns referring to the Trinity are capitalized; satan's names are not.

I dedicate this book to

ישוע

Yeshua (Jesus)
our Messiah, Savior, and Lord
who gave His life for everyone,
including every Muslim;
and who gave me this book
out of my prayer time with Him.

TABLE OF CONTENTS

"If only Yishma'el
could live in Your presence!"
... "I will make him fruitful
and give him many descendants.
He will father twelve princes,
and I will make him a great nation!"
(Gen. 17:20 CJB)

NOTE: Except for the titles, this book will use the Hebrew spellings that give the proper Hebrew pronunciation for most of the Biblical names. The English spelling will be given in paraenthesis the first couple times.

Yeshua is Jesus

Yishma'el is Ishmael

Yitzkhak is Isaac

Avraham is Abraham

Yosef is Joseph

Be'er Sheva is Beer Sheba

Moshe is Moses

HaMashiakh is the Messiah

Ruakh HaKodesh is the Holy Spirit

Ruakh is Spirit (which also means "*wind*")

ha-satan is satan

(which actually means "*the adversary*")

1
GOD SPOKE TO HAGAR

One day after hearing about yet another similarity between Ultra Orthodox Jewish people and non-radical Muslim communities, I began to wonder what it would be like if both communities world-wide came to the Lord! Just think about it. The witness to the world would be so astounding! After all, they are both sons of Avraham!! When they both come to the Lord as a whole, what an amazing united force they will be for God's Kingdom!!! Hallelujah!

Actually just the Muslims alone coming to the Lord would in itself be a very powerful witness to the whole world. Maybe it would be even more powerful since the media and liberals today are more accepting of and sympathetic toward Muslims (Palestinians in particular) than they are toward Christians or Jewish people!!!

Just think about it! It could be a possibility that the Muslims as a group become a witness for the Lord. After all, Yishma'el (Ishmael) did have promises given to him from God. He, too, was saved from death by God as Yitz'khak (Isaac) was! The thought of it got me so excited and overwhelmed that I began to pray earnestly for Muslims.

Soon God began to show me astounding things about His plans for the descendants of Yishma'el, which I will now attempt to show you! Let's start from the very beginning with Sarah's slave, Hagar, Yishma'el's (Ishmael's) mother.

God Himself spoke directly to Hagar, which in itself is amazing! This only happened to a few, select people in the Old Testament. And what is

9

even more amazing is that God didn't just speak to her once! He spoke to her twice and provided for her with a miracle! The first time God spoke to her was when she was pregnant and ran away. He spoke to her about Yishma'el. It could have been Yeshua/Jesus Himself who spoke to her because it says "the angel of Adonai" (the Lord). Some people say that every time the Scripture says "the angel of the Lord" it is an appearance of Yeshua Himself!

> Genesis 16:7-12 (CJB) *The angel of Adonai found her by a spring in the desert, the spring on the road to Shur, and said, "Hagar, Sarai's slave-girl, where have you come from and where are you going? ... Go back to your mistress and submit to her authority. ... I will greatly increase your descendants; there will be so many that it will be impossible to count them. ... You will give birth to a son. You are to call him Yishma'el [God pays attention] because Adonai has paid attention to your misery.*
>
> *He will be a wild donkey of a man with his hand against everyone and everyone's hand against him living his life at odds with all his kinsmen."*

Notice what God is promising her. "I will GREATLY increase your descendants; there will be so many that it will be IMPOSSIBLE to count them!!" The next words sound very similar to the words given about Yeshua to Yosef (Joseph). "*She will give birth to a son and you are to name Him, Yeshua, [which means 'Adonai saves,'] because He will save His people from their sins* " (Matt. 1:21 CJB). In fact, this is one of only four times in Scripture when God told the parents what to name their baby! And Yishma'el is one of them!

The angel of the Lord also foretold Samson's birth and gave instructions of how to raise him, but didn't give his name (Judges 13). God named Yitz'khak (Isaac which means laughter), but didn't give any explanation as to why He chose that name (Gen. 17:19). To the other three, Yokhanan (John), Yeshua (Jesus) and Yishma'el, God gave names that contains His (God's) Name. According to the Strong's Concordance, here are their meanings: Yishma'el [H3458 *"Jehovah pays attention"*], Yokhanan (John)

[H3110 *"from 3076 Jehovah favored, from 2603 … be gracious … have pity upon"*], and Yeshua (Jesus) [H3442 *"He will save, from 3091 Jehovah saved"*]! And it was for only two of them, Yishma'el and Yeshua, that God gave an explanation as to why He was giving that specific name.

Now let's look at the definite, strategic importance of three of these four men named by God. Yitz'khak (Isaac) was the beginning of the bloodline through which the Messiah would be born. Yokhanan (John) was a very important figure in preparing the way for the Messiah. And Yeshua IS the Messiah—the Son of God—the most important person in the universe! With these three persons being so vitally important, surely Yishma'el, the only other person in the Bible named by God, is also important. Surely it has some kind of significance for his descendants! At the very least, they can take comfort and be reassured in the promise that God is "paying attention" and noticing everything that is happening to them!

After God spoke to Hagar, He spoke about Yishma'el to Avraham (Abraham). Avraham said to God, *"If only Yishma'el could live in Your presence!"* God answered, *"…But as for Yishma'el, I have heard you. I have blessed him. I will make him fruitful and give him many descendants. He will father twelve princes, and I will make him a great nation"* (Gen. 17:18, 20 CJB). Keep in mind this specific request by Avraham for Yishma'el because we'll come back to it later.

The second time God spoke to Hagar was when she was banished by Sarah.

> (Gen. 21:11-21 CJB) *Avraham became very distressed over this matter of his son. But God said to Avraham. "Don't be distressed because of the boy and your slave-girl. Listen to everything Sarah says to you…. But I will also make a nation from the son of the slave-girl, since he is descended from you."*
>
> *Avraham got up early in the morning, took bread and a skin of water and gave it to Hagar, putting it on her shoulder, and the child; then he sent her away. After leaving, she wandered in the desert around Be'er-Sheva. When the water in the skin was gone, she left the child under a bush, and went and sat down, looking the other way, about a bow-shot's distance from him; because she*

11

said, "I can't bear to watch my child die." So she sat there, looking the other way, crying out and weeping. God heard the boy's voice, and the angel of God called to Hagar from heaven and said to her, "What's wrong with you, Hagar? Don't be afraid, because God has heard the voice of the boy in his present situation. Get up, lift the boy up, and hold him tightly in your hand, because I am going to make him a great nation." Then God opened her eyes, and she saw a well of water. So she went, filled the skin with water and gave the boy water to drink.

God was with the boy, and he grew. He lived in the desert and became an archer. He lived in the Pa'ran Desert, and his mother chose a wife for him from the land of Egypt.*

The angel spoke to her from heaven this time! She heard a voice from the sky! We would feel amazingly blessed to have such a thing happen to us! I would! Wouldn't you? The voice also spoke her name. How personal and touching is that? It would melt my heart to a puddle! The Lord cared about Hagar and Yishma'el! He cared enough to speak personally to them and to save their lives.

Yitz'khak's (Isaac's) life was spared on the altar by God's voice to Avraham. Yishma'el's life was spared by the angel of God's voice to Hagar.

The angel says God heard Yishma'el's voice. Yishma'el would have been a young man at this time. [He got circumcised when he was 13 in Genesis 17:24 when Avraham was 99 years old. Yitz'khak (Isaac) was born when Avraham was 100.] So what God heard from Yishma'el, who was possibly a 15-year-old, was surely more than just the crying and weeping of a child. Perhaps Yishma'el was praying to God the way Avraham had lovingly taught him during those first 13 years while Avraham still believed that Yishma'el was going to be his only son.

This could be true because notice that Yishma'el believed in God at age 13 to the point of submitting to the command of being painfully circumcised. At that age, this pain would have been quite traumatic. And at age 13 surely he could have refused the operation.

2

BE'ER-SHEVA: MIRACLE WATER FROM A MIRACLE WELL

The well that God showed Hagar, that saved Yishma'el's life must have been a miraculous well. The words, "*God opened her eyes, and she saw a well of water*," make me think of the time God "*opened the eyes*" of Elisha's servant so he could see the whole army of heaven surrounding them (2 Kings 6:17). I think the well Hagar saw wasn't there before. I believe it was a miracle well that God created just at that moment.

So, to me, it looks like Yishma'el was saved by miraculous water. I have heard that the Jews believe it is miracle blood that flows in their veins, since Yitz'khak was conceived miraculously by an elderly couple far beyond child-producing age. Well, something similar could possibly be said about Yishma'el's descendants, since his life was spared by miracle water from a miracle well.

That miracle well, it says in Genesis 21:14, was near Be'er-Sheva (Beer Sheba). This is the first mention of Be'er-Sheva ever in Scripture! And it's when Hagar and Yishma'el are wandering there! But there is more in Scripture about the well that saved Yishma'el's life. Immediately after the story about Yishma'el and Hagar in Genesis, it talks about another well, explaining how the area got its name. Could it possibly be the same well?

Gen. 21:25-34 (CJB) *Now Avraham had complained to Avimelekh (Abimelech) about a well which Avimelekh's servants had seized. Avimelekh answered, "I don't know who has done this. You didn't tell me, and I heard about it only today." Avraham took sheep and cattle and gave them to Avimelekh, and the two of them made a covenant. Abraham put seven female lambs from the flock by themselves. Avimelekh asked Avraham, "What is the meaning of these seven female lambs you have put by themselves?" He answered, "you are to accept these seven female lambs from me as witness that I dug this well." This is why that place was called Be'er-Sheva [well of seven, well of an oath]—because they both swore an oath there. When they made the covenant at Be'er-Sheva, Avimelekh departed with Pikhol that commander of his army and returned to the land of the P'lishtim (Philistines). Avraham planted a tamarisk tree in Be'er-Sheva, and there he called on the Name of ADONAI, the everlasting God. Avraham lived for a long time as a foreigner in the land of the P'lishtim (Philistines).*

I like to think this is the same well that saved Yishma'el. There's no doubt it is a very important well to Avraham. He says he dug it, but he might not want to say that God dug it to a man that has no regard for or belief in God.

Be'er-Sheva (H884 in Strong's Concordance) means *"well of an oath."* Be'er בְּאֵר (H875) means *"a pit, a well."* (Blue Letter Bible online adds *"spring."*) Sheva שֶׁבַע (H7651) means *"seven … indefinite number."* It's from H7650 which means *"to be complete, swear an oath, to feed to the full."*

So, Be'er-Sheva is where God met Hagar and made a promise (similar to an <u>oath</u>) to her. Then immediately after that, it is where Avraham made an <u>oath</u> with a Philistine king and dwelt in peace with him. He planted a tree and called on the Name of the Lord there. In Genesis 22:19 we also see that Avraham returned to Be'er-Sheva after almost sacrificing Yitz'khak.

In Genesis 26:23-25 we read that the Lord appeared to Yitz'khak at Be'er-Sheva. He dug a well there (the last of many wells he dug), made peace with the same Philistine king, Abimelech, and found water in the well at that moment.

Ya'akov (Jacob) apparently grew up in Be'er-Sheva. It was mmediately after the first time he ever left Be'er-Sheva that he saw the ladder with the angel's ascending and descending on it (Gen. 28). Many years later, when Yosef (Joseph) invited his family to move to Egypt for relief from the famine, Ya'akov (Jacob) stopped in Be'er-Sheva to sacrifice to the Lord (Gen. 46).

The tribe of Shimon (Simeon) settled there. "Shimon" (H8095) comes from the root word "shma" שׁמע (H8085). (Keep this in mind for later.) King Joash's mother was from Be'er-Sheva (2 Kings 12:1).

Elijah fled from Jezebel to Be'er-Sheva, then went a days journey into the desert. There an angel fed him and sent him to Mt. Horeb, the Mount of God (I Kings 19:3). (We will come back to the "Mount of God" later.)

Be'er-Sheva is mentioned twice in Amos in a bad light, telling people not to go there, that they shall fall and never rise again.

Just 50 km south of Be'er-Sheva, we find the Nabatean ruins. No one knows the origin of these people who were camel caravan traders, but in Genesis 37:25 (KJV) we read about Ishmaelites (Yishma'elim in Hebrew) coming from Gilead in a caravan with their camels bringing spices, balm, and myrrh to sell in Egypt. (We talk about this caravan again in chapter four.) In I Chronicles 25:30 we see that one of David's civic officials over the camels was Obil, the Ishmaelite. Yishma'el's oldest son's name is Nabaioth. (The "th" is pronounced like a "t.") This name sounds so similar to the Nabatean name that it isn't too hard to imagine that Nabaioth's descendants, at least some of them, were called Nabateans.

After centuries of the Nabateans being camel caravan traders, the Roman shipping by sea made their business extinct. So, near Be'er-Sheva is where they settled and became wine producers. What's exciting is that their whole society came to know Yeshua from the preaching and healing of an evangelist from Bethlehem in the fourth century AD. All this at Be'er Sheva with descendants of Yishma'el!

Also in the desert near Be'er-Sheva, there is an oasis in a beautiful gorge called Nahal Zin (in Ein Avdat National Park). Monks lived in caves there during the Dark Ages in order to get away from corrupt society and live in purity for the Lord.

Today Be'er-Sheva is in the West Bank under the control of the Palestinians (which comes from the word "Philistine"). And many Jewish people still live there. [Avraham, the Jewish ancestor made peace with Abimelech a Philistine at this very same place.] The Gaza War of January 2009 started because the Kassam rockets that had been launched by Palestinians from Gaza into Israel for years, hitting the small town of S'derot, began to reach Be'er-Sheva. These Kassam attacks began soon after Israel pulled out of Gaza in 2004. From then on the people of S'derot had been living a life of terror, having to take shelter, sometimes several times a day, whenever the bomb alert sirens went off. Houses were damaged, people were hurt, and a few were killed, yet the Israeli government didn't do much about it all those years. It was when the rockets began to reach Be'er Sheva that the Israeli government decided enough was enough.

Now let's delve further into the meaning of the name, Be'er Sheva. "Be'er" בְּאֵר (H875) comes from the root word בָּאַר (H874) which means "*to dig, to explain, to declare, to make plain.*" (Blue Letter Bible online at blueletterbible.org adds: "*to make distinct and clear, to engrave, letters on a tablet.*") What does "engraved, letters on a tablet" make us think of? The Ten Commandments! The Word!! The Word of God makes everything "distinct and clear"!! How interesting!

All of this makes me think there is some great significance to Be'er-Sheva. It is a place that is significant for "calling on the Lord" and being blessed by the Lord. And it somehow speaks of Yishma'el's descendants—the Palestinians and Arabs making true shalom with Israel.

Lord, we pray that what took place at Be'er-Sheva in the past will happen again. May both Yishma'el's and Yitz'khak's descendants come to know the Shalom that comes from meeting You and "calling on Your Name," and may they come to know the blessing of making an oath of shalom with their long lost brother!

And Lord, we pray that they will both drink from Your Be'er (well) of Living Water, and learn from Your Words engraved on Your tablet that make everything clear and distinct, and thus may they be made complete in You.

3
ISHMAELITES AND MIDIANITES

Yosef (Joseph) was sold to Ishmaelites! The camel caravan people that bought him were Ishmaelites!! We see this in Genesis 37:26-27 *"What profit is it if we kill our brother ...? Come, let us sell him to the Ishmaelites...."* Genesis 39:1 says that Potiphar, an officer of Pharaoh—captain of the guard, bought him from the Ishmaelites. So, it was Ishmaelites that saved Yosef (Joseph)! If that caravan had not come along, his brothers would have killed him! God obviously ordained that Yosef be saved. And God chose Ishmaelites to do the saving!! So, without Yishma'el's descendants, the Jewish ancestors, including Yeshua's ancestor, would've starved in the famine because Yosef wouldn't have been in Egypt to rescue the world from it! So, it looks like Yishma'el's descendants deserve some gratitude!!

In Genesis 37:28,36 Ishmaelites are called Midianites. Now, apparently not all Midianites were Ishmaelites because one of Avraham's sons from his second wife, Keturah, was named Midian.

In Judges 8:24 the Ishmaelites and Midianites are spoken of as very similar people. And we find out that they could be identified by the jewelry and clothing they wore: golden earrings, crescents, pendants, and their purple, royal garments; also by the collars on the necks of their camels. Did you notice the word "crescents"? What is the symbol of the Islam religion today? None other than a crescent moon! The Arab world's version of the

Red Cross is a Red Crescent! This seems to me like a bit of proof that Arabs today are descendants of Yishma'el.

Moshe (Moses) married the daughter of the priest of Midian (Ex. 2:16). We will talk about Moshe's father-in-law later because this has great significance.

There are some negative things about the Midianites, as I'm sure you are already aware. Here's just one example: the Midianites were involved with wanting Balaam to curse the Israelites. Balak, the king, sent the elders of Midian along with the elders of Moab (Lot's descendants) to employ Balaam (Numbers 22:4,7).

4

KEDAR AND BEDOUINS

Yishma'el's second son's name is Kedar. In the concordance (H6938), it says that his descendants were collectively known as Bedouins (spelled "bedawin" in the concordance). When we were in Israel, my husband and I had the privilege of going to a Bedouin museum and meeting some Bedouins. We got to sit in a Bedouin tent where a Bedouin man made their special, powerfully strong coffee and explained their culture. He told us that unlike the Muslims, Bedouins believe that a person can pray anywhere in any direction because God is everywhere.

The Bedouin religion is much older than Islam. The Bedouins believe in the God of Avraham. The culture's favorite story is the Biblical account of when the three angels visited Avraham. Now, how would they know that story unless Yishma'el and Hagar had told them? To me this is one of several things that signify that, amazingly, Yishma'el continued to believe in God and worship God even after he was banished from his father and his home. But this shouldn't surprise us. Remember that Avraham prayed that Yishma'el would live in the Lord's presence. Also there's a possibility that Avraham reconciled with him later. (See p. 33.)

My husband, later on, had the awesome opportunity to eat in the modern home of a modern, Bedouin, extended family. He discovered that they identify themselves politically with the Arabs in Israel (who since 1967 call themselves Palestinians). To me, that is most likely because they are all descendants of Yishma'el.

Isaiah mentions the Bedouins!

Isaiah 42: 10-11 *Sing to the LORD a new song, His praise from the end of the earth! ... Let the desert and its towns lift up their voice, the villages that Kedar inhabits ... sing, let them shout from the tops of the mountains. Let them give glory to the LORD, and declare His praise....*

Yes, Lord, please bring this to pass. May the descendants of Kedar, Yishma'el's son, the Bedouins, come to know You and be so filled with the JOY of Your salvation that they will sing praises to You and will shout out their testimonies from the mountain tops, giving You all the Glory! Amen! Hallelujah!!

5

THE SIGNIFICANCE OF WHERE YISHMA'EL SETTLED

Yishma'el lived in the wilderness of Paran (Gen. 21:21). *"His descendants settled from Havilah to Shur, which is opposite Egypt in the direction of Assyria"* (Gen. 25:18). Havilah is mentioned in Genesis 2:11-12. *"The river Pishon flows around the whole land of Havilah where there is good gold, bdellium and onyx stone."*

Onyx stone is a stone of authority. It is worn on the High Priest's shoulders. To me that is very interesting—something to ponder, that Yishma'el's descendants settled where there was good gold and gems, including the gem of authority.

That's where his descendants settled which is significant enough, but the place where Yishma'el himself lived, the wilderness of Paran, is of even more significance to me. Paran is mentioned in Habakkuk.

Habakkuk 3:3-7 *God came from Teman* (Teman was a grandson of Esau.) *the Holy One from Mt. Paran. Selah. His Glory covered the heavens, and the earth was full of His praise. The brightness was like the sun; rays came forth from His hands where His power lay hidden. ... He stopped and shook the earth.... The eternal mountains were shattered.... The tent-curtains of the land of Midian trembled.*

Do you suppose this Mt. Paran could be Mt. Sinai? Yes, it could! It is actually the very same mountain! Look at Deuteronomy 33:2 *"The Lord* came from Sinai, and dawned from Seir upon us; He shone forth from Mount Paran."

To me, the fact that Yishma'el lived near Mt. Sinai is very important. For one thing, it is another of the many facts that support my notion that Yishma'el continued to worship God the way he had been taught by his father, even after his father exiled him, even in this place called Paran.

Paran פָּארָן (H6286) (pronounced pa'ar) means *"to gleam, … to explain (i.e. to make clear) oneself."* It is from (H6288) *"to shake a tree; beautify … glorify self."* This is exactly what God did at Mt. Sinai. He <u>gleamed</u> brightly, <u>shook</u> the mountain, <u>revealed</u> His <u>Glory</u>, and <u>explained</u> Himself.

This region was named Paran long before Moses. The first time in Scripture that any name of the region or mountain is mentioned is when it is talking about Yishma'el settling there. So, perhaps God was revealing Himself at that mountain as far back as Yishma'el! For all we know, Yishma'el could have been the one who gave the place its name!

6
REUEL—JETHRO,
A PRIEST

Let me explain my reasoning for Yishma'el's faithfulness further. Yishma'el's daughter, Basamath, who married Esau, named her son Reuel (Gen. 36:3,10). "Reuel" רעואל (H7467) means *"friend of God."*

As proof that Basamath had something to do with naming her son, let's look at Esau's other sons' names from his two other Canaanite wives: Eliphaz (H464) *"god of gold"*; Jeush (H3266) *"hasty"*; Jaalam (H3281) *"occult"*; and Korah (H7141) *"ice."* That's quite a difference in meanings from *"friend of God"*! None of them have to do with the One, True God at all. In fact, two of them have to do with false gods. These are all wives of Esau and he either named his sons these names himself or allowed his wives to name them thus. Unless Esau had a complete change of heart, it was Basamath, his newest wife, who chose the "new" thing of honoring God with the name of her son. If Esau ever had a change of heart, it was much later when he went to meet Ya'akov (Jacob).

Moshe's (Moses') father-in-law's name was Reuel (Ex. 2:18 NRSV). Jethro was his title because "Jethro" (H3503) means *"his excellence."* Possibly, since he was a Midianite and lived near Mt. Paran, he was a descendant of Yishma'el. If so, then possibly he was named after his ancestor, Reuel, Yishma'el's grandson.

Reuel was a priest. I believe he was a priest of the One, True God. Why? In Exodus 3:1 we read that Moses led his sheep beyond the wilderness and came to Horeb, the mountain of God. ("Horeb" is yet another name for Mt. Sinai!) Now, how did Moses know it was the "mountain of

God" unless Reuel had told him? Perhaps it is just the writer of Exodus identifying this as the mountain of the Lord. But, perhaps not. Perhaps Reuel truly knew the Lord. Perhaps belief in God had been passed down to him from his ancestor, Yishma'el. Perhaps, as mentioned before, Yishma'el had also met the Lord when he lived near this very same mountain.

So, this is the mountain where God chose to reveal Himself to Moshe in the burning bush and later to the whole nation of Israel. It is also the mountain where God took Elijah after Elijah had proven that God was the Almighty on Mt. Carmel, had killed 400 prophets of Baal, but then fled from Jezebel. You would think God could've chosen any spot to encourage Elijah, but He didn't. He specifically took Elijah far away to Mt. Horeb. There, God's presence was preceded by the same things as at the time of the Ten Commandments: rocks breaking in pieces, earthquake, and fire (I Kings 19:11).

To me, this all shows that Mt Paran/Sinai/Horeb is a very special mountain where God revealed Himself to people, and that perhaps Yishma'el met God at this mountain, too. If so, it would have just been God answering Avraham's prayer that Yishma'el could live in God's presence (Gen. 17:20)! And we know that God answers prayer!! I will give you more reasons to believe this about Yishma'el later. But right now let me show you that Reuel worshipped the Lord.

> Exodus 18:10-11 Jethro said, "Blessed be the LORD, who has delivered you from the Egyptians and from Pharaoh. Now I know that the LORD is greater than all gods, because he delivered the people from the Egyptians, when they dealt arrogantly with them." And Jethro, Moses' father-in-law, brought a burnt offering and sacrifices to God; and Aaron came with all the elders of Israel to eat bread with Moses' father-in-law in the presence of God.

You could say that Jethro didn't know the Lord until that moment because he says, "Now I know that the LORD (HaShem) is greater than all gods." But we could also say that he knew God, but he was unsure about this God that Moses was calling by a different name than Jethro had heard before. My theory is supported by the fact that Jethro knew how to worship God. He knew that God required burnt offerings and sacrifices. And Jethro's sacrifices brought the presence of the Lord. It says that they ate "*in the presence God.*" It wasn't Moses or Aaron who did the sacrificing in this incident. It was Jethro/Reuel, who was also leading the whole ceremony, it appears. He was perhaps a long-time worshipper of God, learned from teachings passed down from Yishma'el who learned them from his father, Avraham.

Now, let's look at some even more exciting things about Yishma'el!

7

THE MEANING OF ISHMAEL'S NAME

The angel told Hagar to name her son Yishma'el because the Lord "paid attention to [her] misery." This was based on the meaning of the name. His name in Hebrew is ישמעאל (H3458 in the concordance). It is a combination of two Hebrew words: אל (H410) which means "*God*" and shma שמע (H8085) which mainly means "*to hear*" or "*listen intelligently (often with the implication of attention…).*"

This word has very important meaning to Jewish people. Every Jewish synagogue meeting begins with the reciting of the "Shma." "*Shma Yisrael Adonai Elohenu Adonai Echad*" "*Hear, O Israel, the Lord our God the Lord is one.*" This is God's Word to Israel through Moses in Deuteronomy 6:4, quoted by Yeshua in Mark 12:29.

We will delve further into the meaning of this word "shma" and talk more about its importance in a minute because one of Yishma'el's sons also contains it and, as mentioned earlier, so does the name of the Jewish tribe, Shimon (Simeon).

O Adonai, You listened to Yishma'el's voice in the wilderness that day and paid attention. May Yishma'el's descendants today be able to shma (hear) You and shma Your Word. May they listen intellegently and pay attention to You and always obey You.

8

THE MEANING OF ISHMAEL'S SONS' NAMES

Yishma'el had twelve sons. Can you believe that? He had twelve sons just like Yaakov (Jacob) did! God promised Avraham he would (Gen. 17:20).

Twelve is a very important number in Scripture. Yeshua chose twelve disciples. Yaakov's (Jacob's) twelve sons are the origin of the twelve tribes of Israel. Yishma'el's twelve sons were the "twelve princes" which were the beginning of the nation God promised He would make from Yishma'el. When God makes a nation, He doesn't do it half-heartedly. He started Israel with twelve sons from one man. He started the New Covenant with twelve disciples. And we see here that He started Yishma'el's nation with twelve sons from him. This astounded me when I first saw it.

The next thing that amazed me was the meanings of Yishma'el's sons' names! Keep in mind that according to Scripture, the meaning of a child's name was very important in that culture. They often named them according to what was happening in their spiritual lives at the time. For example, Yosef (Joseph) named his oldest son M'nasheh (Manasseh) (H4519) which means *"causing to forget"* because God had helped him to forget his painful past (Gen. 41:51). Yitz'khak (which means *"laughter"*) was named thus because his miraculous existence brought so much joy—just the thought of him being born made Sarah and Avraham laugh (Gen. 17:17 and 18:12).

So, here are Yishma'el's sons' names from Genesis 25:12-18.

1. Nebaioth (N'vayot in CJB) (H5032) נְבָיוֹת *"fruitfulness."* It's from 5107 נוב nav *"germinate, to flourish (also of words), utter: —bring forth fruit, make cheerful, increase"*

The Hebrew word "naveh" (H5029) נָבִיא means prophet. The plural—prophets—would be navehot which is almost exactly the same as Nevaoth (N'vayot), also a plural word. The root of naveh (prophet) is H5012 נבא neva which means *"prophesy, i.e. speak (or sing) by inspiration..."* So the two words don't have the exact same root but they sound the same and even the meanings of the roots have a connection. When a person is prophesying they are "uttering," and their words are "flourishing."

2. Kedar (H6938) קֵדָר *"dusky (of the skin or the tent); Kedar, a son of Ishmael; also (collect.) bedawin (as his descendants or representatives)."* It is from H6937 a prim. root; *"to be ashy, i.e. dark-colored; by impl. To mourn (in sackcloth or sordid garments): —be black ... mourn."*

3. Adbeel (Adbe'el in CJB) (H110) אַדְבְּאֵל *"from 109 [אדב adab which means 'languish, grieve'] (in the sense of chastisement)"* and from H410 אֵל *"the Almighty ... God."* So the complete meaning is "disciplined of God."

4. Mibsam (Mivsam in CJB) (H4017) *"from the same as 1314 basem, fragrant, spicy, also the balsam plant."*

5. Mishma (H4927) *"same as 4926 'a report, —hearing. From 8085 shma שָׁמַע.'"* The word שָׁמַע has a long list of meanings. Here is a shortened list of them: *"to hear intelligently (often with the implication of attention, obedience, etc....) discern, give ear, ... hear, ... listen, ... perceive, proclaim, publish, ... report, ... understand, witness."* This is the same word, "shma," which is in the middle of Yishma'el's name יִשְׁמָעֵאל.

This "shma" is also the whole meaning of Shimon's (Simeon's) name who is Ya'akov's (Jacob's) second son [8095 שִׁמְעוֹן Shimone]. Reuben, Ya'akov's eldest son's name partly means "to see." So, God wanted the Israelites to both see and hear Him!! The New Testament name, Simon, is the Greek translation of the Hebrew name, Simeon. So this "shma" makes up two of Yeshua's disciples' names: Simon Peter and Simon, the Zealot.

I find this very interesting! The Lord really wants us to listen to Him—to perceive, understand, obey, and proclaim Him!

6. Dumah (H1746) דּוּמָה *same as 1745 'from an unused root—to be dumb, silence, fig. death—silence (Compare 1820)'" damah* דָּמָה *"a prim. root; to be dumb or silent; hence to fail or perish; trans. To destroy: —cease, be cut down (off), destroy, be brought to silence, be undone, x utterly."*

An interesting aside is that the Hebrew word (H1818) דָּם [dam ("a" as in father)] means *"blood (as that which when shed causes death) ... by analogy the juice of the grape; ... bloodshed (i.e. drops of blood); ... + innocent."* The word "dam" is a primary root that is from H1826 דָּמַם (damam) which has almost the exact same as 1820 דָּמָה (damah) (See above.). Here is the meaning of H1826 דָּמַם (damam): *"to be dumb, ... to be astonished, to stop; also to perish: —cease, be cut down (off), forbear, hold peace, quiet self, rest, be silent, keep (put to) silence, be (stand) still, tarry, wait."*

I found it interesting to note that Yeshua was silent or dumb (dumah or damam) before his killers as He was shedding His blood (dam). But then I looked up Isaiah 53:7 and found that the word used for "dumb" there is not damam or dumah, but H481 אָלַם alam which means *"to bind, to be dumb, to be bound, binding."* He was bound and dumb for us so that we can be set free and can speak forth His Truth to the world. "World" in Hebrew sounds similar: (H5769) עֹלָם olam! This is fascinating to me!

7. Massa (H4854) *"burden, from 4853 'burden, tribute, portage, fig. an utterance, chiefly a doom, espec. singing; ... burden, carry away, prophecy...'"*

8. Hadad (H1924) הֲדַד (Hadar) *"same as 1926 'magnificence, i.e. ornament or splendor—beauty, excellency, glorious, glory, goodly, honor, majesty.'"*

9. Tema (Teima in CJB) (H8485) תֵּמָא *"probably of foreign derivative."* תֵּימָן (H8486) means *"from the south."* According to the book, *Hebrew Word Pictures: How does the Hebrew Alphabet Reveal Prophetic Truths?* by Dr. Frank T. Seekins, the letter "tav" ת in Hebrew means *"a mark, a sign."* The way it was originally written, it looked like a cross. So, it signifies the sign of the Lord's cross. The letter symbolizes ownership; *"to seal; to make a covenant; to join two things together; to make a sign"* (p. 96).

29

10. Jetur (Y'tur in CJB) (H3195) יְטוּר yetur *"encircled (i.e. enclosed) probably from 2905 tur 'from an unused root to range, in a regular manner; a row; hence a wall.'"*

11. Naphish (Nafish in CJB) (H5305) *"refreshed from 5314 naphash 'to breath, to be breathed upon, i.e. refreshed (as if by a current of air) ....'"*

12. Kedemah (Kedmah in CJB) (H6929) קְדְמָה *"precedence from 6923 qadam 'a prim. root: to project (oneself) i.e. precede; hence to antici-pate, hasten, meet (usually for help) ....meet, prevent.'"*

His daughter's name is Bashemath (H1315) which like Mibsam also means *"fragrant."*

Here's a summary list of the meanings:

- Fruitful, flourish in words, utter (prophesy)
- Dusky, dark, mourn in sackcloth
- Chastised or disciplined of God
- Fragrance (also his daughter's name)
- Hear and obey, discern, give ear, listen, understand, report, declare
- Silence, destroy, be brought to silence
- Burden, utterance, carry away, prophecy
- Magnificence, glory, glorious, majesty
- Sign (of the cross), joining two things together
- Encircled, enclosed, a row, a wall
- Refreshed from a breeze, breathed upon
- Precedent, anticipate, hasten, meet, prevent

I was amazed that Yishma'el gave his sons names with these kinds of meanings. Why do you suppose he chose each of those names? What could he have been going through that caused him to choose those meanings? Well, this is what I see. At first Yishma'el was flourishing and felt hopeful. Then perhaps he began <u>mourning </u>his separation from his father. Prosper-ity couldn't erase that.

Perhaps he was also <u>mourning</u> with the sorrow of repentance before God as many of us do in the middle of our adulthood when we start to see things in a new light. As a result, perhaps he realized that he deserved to be <u>chastised of God</u>, as we all deserve. Then out of that repentance came the time of sensing God's wonderful <u>fragrant</u> presence. He sensed this <u>fragrance</u> so much he gave two children that name. Then his ears were opened to truly <u>hear</u> God's voice—to <u>listen intently</u> and to begin to really <u>understand</u> and <u>perceive</u> what God was saying, with his own full <u>intention of obeying</u> the Lord.

He was brought to <u>silence</u> as he listened. He sat in <u>silent</u> awe of the Creator. His <u>burden</u> of feelings of rejection and resentment were <u>carried away</u> as he beheld the <u>majesty</u> of the Lord and was <u>encircled</u> by His love, <u>refreshed</u> by the <u>breath</u> of God and by the longing to <u>meet</u> Him.

That is my take on the reason for the meanings of the names. I love thinking that it is true, even though it is only a hypothesis.

Also, perhaps some of Yishma'el's <u>refreshing</u> feelings of release came after he <u>met</u> Avraham again. I believe Avraham reconciled with Yishma'el. Here's why. According to Scripture, Avraham had only two women besides Sarah: Hagar and Keturah. In Genesis 25:6 it says Avraham gave gifts to the sons of his concubines. Since the word "concubines" is plural, it must mean that he gave gifts to Yishma'el, too. This means that at some point Avraham found out where Yishma'el was and re-connected with him—without a cell phone or facebook!! This would've taken a lot of effort on Avraham's part!! We do know that Avraham loved Yishma'el dearly and did not want to send him away. Could it be that he said something like the following to Yishma'el? "Look, Son. I don't want to send you away, but God has instructed me to do so. Be brave, Son. God is going to take care of you, and as soon as I can, I will come and see you." Perhaps there was a lot of contact once Yitz'khak was old enough for Sarah to feel he was safe. One thing is sure, in the end we see Yitz'khak and Yishma'el together at Avraham's death. Together, they bury their father (Gen. 25:9-10). As I read that I sense lots of love and reconciliation.

One thing we know absolutely for sure is that God is in control of all things. Therefore, God was ultimately in control of what Yishma'el's sons were named. So, if we look at it that way, we can see prophecy in those names—some of which has already come to pass.

Yishma'el certainly <u>flourished</u> in having twelve sons who became princes. Then we know from the Bible that the Midianites were "<u>chastised</u>

of God" and "silenced and destroyed" to some degree by Gideon's army. Not much is said later on in Scripture about Arab history.

We see from post Biblical history that for a time the Arab culture did grow and conquer until it became "magnificent." (Our English alphabet and many of our mathematical theorems came from the Arabs.) After the Roman and Byzantine empires fell, the Arabs ruled the Middle East and was "glorious" from 638 A.D. until 1917 in World War I. (The Dome of the Rock was built in 691 A.D.) There were several dynasties. Among them are: the Omayyad dynasty; the Seljuk Turks; ruler, Saladin, and the Ayyubid dynasty; the Marmelukes; and ruler, Suleyman the Magnificent of the Ottoman Turks. This history appears to fulfill God's promise that from Yishma'el He would make "a great nation."

Today Arabs and Jews are living "together" in one land. Many of those Arabs (who only since 1967 began calling themselves Palestinians) are "encircled and enclosed" by "walls."

That's where it looks like we are now in the prophecy of Yishma'el's sons' names. The rest is still to come.

If these names are a prophecy, then the Arabs and Muslims are soon to see the sign of the cross, and to be "breathed upon" by the refreshing breeze of the Ruakh HaKodesh (Holy Spirit). Actually we are seeing the beginnings of that happen. Many Muslims are being visited in their dreams by Yeshua. They are coming to believe in Yeshua (or "Issa" as they call Him) in greater and greater numbers all over the Middle East and beyond! It is very exciting to us, but very worrying to the Muslim leaders!

Next, according to the meaning of the names, it looks like having the Muslims come to faith in Yeshua will "hasten" the day when we will "meet" the Lord in the air, and the army of heaven will conquer, "preventing" the kingdom of darkness from taking over the earth.

When I first saw this as a prophecy and how some of it has already been fulfilled, I got chills up and down my back—chills of anticipation and excitement. The coming of the Lord is surely very near!! It could happen in my lifetime!

Lord God of Heaven above, I pray this IS a prophecy for Arabs today, and I pray it will come to pass!!

32

9
"WITHIN
THE YEAR" PRAYER

I had asked the Lord to reveal His plan for the Muslims to me. His answer was to give me the driving desire to study the meaning of Yishma'el's sons' names. After that the Lord began giving me Scriptures to turn into intercessory prayers to pray for the Arabs and Muslims. Here's the first one. I put my comments and Hebrew meanings in brackets [ ].

Isaiah 21:6-16 (KJV) For thus hath the Lord said unto me, Go set a watchman, Let him declare what he seeth. And he saw

A chariot with a couple horsemen, [The most beautiful breed of horses is the Arabian! On Ramadan, the West Bank streets are filled with horses instead of cars. (But, of course, all kinds of people are horsemen!)]

A chariot of asses [or donkeys], [God told Hagar that Yishma'el would be a "wild donkey of a man."]

A chariot of camels, [Ishmaelites were known for their camels.]

And he hearkened diligently with much heed.

And he cried, A lion: [Yeshua is called a lion.]

Verse 8 My Lord, I stand continually upon the watchtower in the daytime and I set in my ward whole nights: and, behold, here cometh a chariot of men, with a couple horsemen. And he answered, Babel is fallen, is fallen; and all her graven images ... broken....

Verses 11-12 The burden [son #7, Massa, means "*burden*"] of Dumah [son #6 means "*to be silenced, to destroy*"]. He calleth to me out of Seir [H8165 "*rough, shaggy ...*"] Watchmen what of the night? ... The watchman said, the morning cometh, and also the night. If ye will inquire, inquire ye. Return, come.

Verses 14-15 The inhabitants of ... Tema [son # 9, sign of the cross] brought water to him that was thirsty. They prevented with their bread, him that fled. For they fled from ... war.

Verses 16-17 For thus hath the Lord said unto me, <u>Within a year</u> according to the years of an hireling, and all the glory of Kedar [son #2 "*mourn in sackcloth*"] shall fail: The mighty men of the children of Kedar shall be diminished. **For the Lord God of Israel hath spoken it.**

Now that you know the names of Yishma'el's sons, you can see how this passage speaks of Yishma'el's descendants! I'm not sure what it all means, but it does look like the descendants of Yishma'el will play a part in the End Times. Some fleeing from war and some, those of the <u>sign of the cross,</u> giving water and bread to those fleeing, perhaps Living Water and the Bread of Life!! Others, it looks like according to this passage, will be the warriors of the war, but they shall fail "within a year."

I underlined the words "within a year" because those words struck me. The Lord used them to speak to me and to give me a command. Before I tell you what that command was, let me tell you what had just occurred in my life. The date was November 12, 2008. I wrote in my journal, "Today the oil prices came down to $56 something a barrel! They say that is the price of oil in the beginning of 2007! So all my prayers for the oil and gas prices to come crashing down that I've been praying since September 2007 are being answered. They started coming down within a year of when I started praying!!!"

"May they keep coming crashing down, Lord," the journal continues, "In Yeshua's Name, I command the gas and oil prices to come crashing down to 2004 levels! May gas come down to $1.25 a gallon!!"

I was so amazed that the Lord was answering my cry. I had been crying out earnestly about the gas prices because my job as a visiting nurse job required a tremendous amount of driving from one side of the huge city to another a few times a day. The price of gas was eating into my income, causing us great financial difficulty.

I had prayed for several months, yet the prices continued to climb. They didn't start coming down until the day my daughter (who came back from graduate school in August) began to agree with me in prayer. And the prices eventually came down very close to what she and I had asked. (The sad thing today, as I write this, is that the prices are starting to creep up again. We all need to pray!!)

There was another prayer that the Lord had just answered miraculously for me at that time. I had visited a friend's church in another state and had become very concerned about the leadership there. I was extremely worried that my friend was getting caught up in a what was becoming very much like a cult group. I said a little bit to her, but not much. Having come out of a cult myself as a young adult, I knew I would only drive a wedge between her and I if I spoke against her leaders whom she held in awe. When I got home I spent much time in grieving prayer about it. Then the Lord gave me the verse, Zechariah 5:1, to use to pray over this situation. It is about the "flying scroll" that God sends out over the face of the whole land that brings a curse that shall enter into the house of anyone who "swears falsely by My Name, and shall abide in that house and consume it both timber and stone."

I began to pray this verse over those church leaders. I prayed that if they were teaching false things in the Name of the Lord, the curse would consume their houses and their church both timber and stone! A few months later, I got a call from my friend telling me that one leader was in jail for molesting his daughter. I was absolutely shocked! He and the top leader were the two I was most concerned about!! Later she told me the top leader was being asked to step down by the church founders, but was refusing, so many families were leaving. The leader's response to all this was exposing his true character which was very controlling and manipulative, causing other people to fear leaving. She said she and her husband were thinking of leaving, too, but they were worried about what he would do to them or to their children, if he knew. In the end, they were able to leave secretly without any trouble. Praise the Lord!!

So, that is the background of the miraculous, faith-building answers to prayer from which God gave me this new command. God told me to now start praying for the demise of Islam—to pray that Islam would diminish and fail "within a year" as the verse says; that it would come crashing down as the gas prices had. So, here is how I began prayng.

I pray for the demise of Islam! In Yeshua's (Jesus') Name, by the Power of YESHUA'S (JESUS') BLOOD, may Islam come crashing down; may Jihad come crashing down—within the year! I command, by the POWER and AUTHORITY of the BLOOD of JESUS for suicide bombing and terrorist attacks to come to an end—for all terrorism to cease.

May the dark ages of Islam be over. May all Muslims come to the LIGHT. May the veil be removed. May they repent in <u>sackcloth</u> and become <u>fragrance</u> unto the Lord. May they <u>hear (shma)</u> Your voice, may they be <u>silenced</u> (Dumah). May they see Your <u>sign, the Cross.</u> May the <u>burden</u> (Massa) of their sins be <u>carried away</u> (also Massa). May they see Your <u>Glory</u> (Hadar). May they be <u>encircled</u> (Y'tur) by Your arms and <u>enclosed</u> (Y'tur) by Your wings, and <u>breathed upon</u> (Naphish) by Your Ruakh HaKodesh (Holy Spirit), and may they <u>hasten</u> (Kedmah) the Day of Your Coming!!

Keep in mind that I didn't see a turn around in the gas prices until someone joined me and we agreed together in prayer. Perhaps the Lord has me writing this because He wants to inspire others to agree with me in praying this prayer, so the answer will come!

10

FOUR
BLACKSMITHS

Next, the Lord led me to Zechariah 1:20-21.

> Then the LORD showed me four blacksmiths. And I asked, "What are they coming to do?" He answered, "These are the horns that scattered Judah, so that no head could be raised; but these have come to terrify them, to strike down the horns of the nations that lifted up their horns against the land of Judah to scatter its people."

> And the LORD shewed me four carpenters. Then said I, What come these to do? And He spake, saying, These are the horns which have scattered Judah so that no man did lift up his head: but these are come to fray them, to cast out the horns of the Gentiles, which lifted up their horn over the land of Judah to scatter it (KJV).

I asked the Lord who these blacksmiths or carpenters are. In the concordance the word is H2796 חָרָשׁ kharash. It means "fabricator of any material." It is from H2790 a primary root meaning "to scratch, to engrave, to devise (secrecy), to be silent, to let alone, to be deaf ... hold peace, plow, ... be quiet, rest ... hold tongue ..."

So, they are craftsman! Perhaps after they do their "terrifying," they will make something beautiful out of those "horns" and those "nations" that they "terrify" and "strike down"!

The word "fray" in the KJV or "terrify" in the NRSV is H2729 חָרַד Kharad. It is a root word which means "to shudder with terror, hence to *fear, also to hasten (with anxiety) – to be (make) afraid, be careful, discomfit, fray (away), quake, tremble.*" I looked up the word "fray" in the American Heritage Dictionary (1978 edition) and found that its obsolete meaning, not obsolete in the 1600's when the King James Version was being written, is "1. *to alarm, frighten.* 2. *to drive away.*" It sounds like we could have gotten our English word "horrid" from it—Kharad—horrid. Can you hear the similarity in sound?

So now I knew that these <u>quiet</u> blacksmiths/fabricators/engravers will "scare away" and "strike down" the enemy in control of these "horns."

The Hebrew word for "strike down" (NRSV) or "cast out" (KJV) is H3034 יָדָה yadah. It means "*to use (i.e. hold out) the hand; phys. to throw (a stone, an arrow) at or away,; espec. to revere or worship (with extended hands); intens. to bemoan (by wringing the hands): cast (out),(make) confess (-ion) ,praise, shoot, (give) thank (-ful), to give praise, to confess (the Name of God), to confess (sin).*" It is from H3027 יָד yad "*hand, strength.*" On the internet at blueletterbible.org, it says the meaning is "*1) to throw, shoot, cast; a) to shoot (arrows); b) to cast, cast down, throw down; c) 1) to give thanks, laud, praise; 2) to confess, confess (the Name of God); d) 1) to confess (sin) 2) to give thanks.*"

Now, the really exciting thing to me was to find out that though this word is used 114 times in 111 verses in the Tanakh (the Old Testament), it is used only once to mean "cast," only once to mean "shoot," and only once right here in Zechariah 1:20 to mean "cast out." All the other times it has something to do with giving praise or thanks or confessing. Fifty-three times it is used to mean "praise" and thirty-five times to refer to "giving thanks" many of which are in the Psalms.

This excited me because, to me, it shows that our battle against the enemy has a lot to do with confessing our sins, confessing God's Name, and giving thanks and praise to God. In other words, our worship IS warfare! When we worship the Lord, we are "terrifying" the enemy! It is scaring him away! Our worship can be used to "cast out" the enemy!! This also implies that our warfare prayers against the enemy should be full of reverence, praise, and thanksgiving to our Lord! And all of this is by the יָד yad—hand—of God!

Even our "bemoaning" or "grieving" as in Ezekiel 9:4-6 can be pleasing to the Lord. "*Go through the city, through Jerusalem, and put a mirk on the foreheads of those who sigh and groan over all the abominations that are committed in it. ... Pass through the city after him and kill; your eye shall not spare, and you shall show no pity. ...but touch no one who has the mark.*" So, our prayers can also include the deep groaning, sighing, and grieving of our heart over the evil we see in the world today.

I looked up the word "horn" also. It is H7161 קֶרֶן qeren "*a horn (as projecting), by impl. a flask, cornet, by resemb. elephant's tooth (i.e. ivory), a corner (of the altar), a peak (of a mountain), a ray (of light), fig. power:* [Blue Letter Bible says *strength*] *hill, horn.*" It is from 7160 קָרַן qaran "*to push or gore.*"

There are many nations or peoples over the centuries that "lifted up their 'horn' (or power) against" Israel to "scatter" them. Most of them have come to nothing. One of the latest groups was the Nazi's. They were defeated. The groups today include the Hamas, the Hezbullah, Al Qaeda, the Taliban, the Fatah, Iran and most of the Arab countries. What do all these have in common? They are all Muslim!

Where does the "horn" or "power" or "strength" of Islam lie? Well, one place is in the Koran. When I realized all this I then took this verse to begin to pray that the power of the Koran be "frayed," "cast out," and "struck down"—that the hold it has over the people will come to an end.

Out of the Koran comes the power of Jihad. Out of Jihad comes terrorism. So, I also began praying for the power of Jihad to come unraveled and be "cast out."

When you look at the Hebrew text of these verses in Zechariah you see that it is made of some similar sounding words. It is sort of a play on words, which is something the Jewish culture loves. Here is how the Hebrew of the main words sound. Arbah (four), kharash (blacksmith/engraver), kharad (to terrify), qeren (horn, power), yadah (cast out), Yehudah (Judah), zarah (scatter).

Here's another interesting thing using another play on words. The word "nations" or "Gentiles" is H1471 גּוֹי goy "*a foreign nation, hence a Gentile, also (fig.) a troop of animals, or a flight of locusts. —Gentile, heathen, nation, people.*" It is from the same root as H1465 גֵּוָה "*the back, the person,* the fem. of 1460 גֵּו, "*the back,*" from H1342 גָּאָה ga'ah "*to mount up, … to rise, (fig.) be majestic; —gloriously, grow up, increase, be risen, triumph.*" This made me think of a similar sounding word H1350 גָּאַל ga'al which means "*to redeem*"!

So, even though these nations that are against Israel are going to be "terrified" and "cast out," the ultimate goal for them (and for all "Gentiles") is to stop turning their <u>backs</u> to the Lord, but instead to trust in the Lord and <u>grow up</u> in Him until they "<u>mount up</u> on wings as eagles" (Isaiah 40:31) and <u>rise</u> up with Him in the air in <u>glory</u> and <u>triumph</u>! The ultimate goal for all of us Gentiles and for Jewish People is that we are <u>redeemed</u>!

11

GILEAD AND LEBANON PRAYER

I also noticed the verse, Zechariah 10:10 *"I will bring them to the land of Gilead and Lebanon until there is no room for them."* NO ROOM for them!!! "Gilead" (H1568) is a combination of two words. The first one means *"a heap of testimony, … a memorial"* and *"something rolled —heap of stones."* The second means *"a witness, testimony."* This brings to mind the time when God told Joshua to tell the priests to bring up stones out of the Jordan river and pile them up as a memorial (Josh. 4:5-7).

The word "Lebanon" (H3844) is also a combination of words which mean *"heart," "comfort, courage, understanding, tenderhearted," "to be (or become) white, to make bricks."* The country Lebanon was named this because of its white, snow-capped mountains. But the actual meaning of the word is basically "hearts made white"!

So, why does God want to bring people to Gilead and Lebanon until there is no more room? Well, it looks to me like God wants there to be a monumental heap of testimonies from an innumerable number of hearts made white by the Blood of Yeshua!! It's talking about Israel here in Zechariah, but we know from the message of the whole Bible that this is God's will for all mankind!

After pondering this, my heart cried out to God. *O Father in heaven, I see now why You tarry so long for Yeshua's Second Coming. You want the heap of testimonies to be higher and higher!! But, please, Father, please bring this to pass. Please let it be fulfilled soon! Please come, Lord, and gather us in. Please bring us to the heap of testimony and of hearts made*

41

white. Bring us all in until there are no more to bring in—until there is no empty room in heaven and until there is no one left out! Please let us begin to enjoy the heap of testimonies from all those down through the ages whose hearts are made white by Yeshua's Blood.

12

BLACKSMITH PRAYERS

I still don't know exactly who these four blacksmiths or craftmen or fabricators are going to be. I have thought that maybe there is one "blacksmith" for each time Israel was scattered or fiercely attacked. They were banished and scattered twice from the land of Israel. And then the Nazi's tried to annihilate them. So there could be just one more "blacksmith." But there are many other times they were severely persecuted, so the numbers wouldn't work out. But I'm not going to worry about it. That is all in the Lord's hands. However, I felt prompted to use all I had learned about the meanings of the Hebrew words in Zechariah 1:20-21 and 10:10 to begin to pray a "Blacksmith" prayer for the Muslims. I also used today's meaning for the word "fray."

Lord, I pray that the religion of Islam will be "cast out." I pray the power of Jihad will be "cast out." I pray it will be <u>frightened</u> away. May a "terrifying" fear come upon all in the Islamic religion, especially on the Jihadists, so "terrifying" that they will abandon Islam and will run to You, Yeshua; that they will cry out to You to be their Savior. I pray the Koran will be "frayed." I pray the power of the Koran will come <u>unraveled</u>. I pray all the power of all the Muslim leaders, especially terrorist leaders and those against Israel, will come completely <u>unraveled</u> and be "cast out."

In יֵשׁוּעַ Yeshua's (Jesus') Name—in You, our crucified and risen Redeemer's Holy Name, may all Muslims quake and tremble before You and bow in reverence and receive You as their Lord and Redeemer.

O Father, You have brought almost every kingdom to an end that has

43

been against Israel. I pray in the Name of Yeshua—by Your un-surpassing Power, that Islam will be brought to an end. I speak in the Name of Yeshua, Islam religion, you come crashing down and be annihilated by the POWER of Yeshua's Name and by the POWER of Yeshua's shed BLOOD!

And I pray that out of Islam there will come a <u>heap of testimonies</u>—a majestic, monumental memorial of <u>testimonies</u> of God's goodness; of God's drawing all Muslims to Himself!!

Lord Yeshua HaMashiakh (the Messiah), bring out the four blacksmith—engravers—designers—that will take the material of Islam and create something new and beautiful which will GLORIFY YOUR NAME!!!!

Later I added more to my praying.

O Lord, I pray for the demise of Islam. In the Power of Yeshua's Name and by the Power of Yeshua's BLOOD, I command Islam to come crashing down! I command Jihad to come crashing down. Be annihilated. Dark ages of Islam, be over! Be DONE!! I pray the LIGHT of God will come to all Muslims. I pray and beg You, Yeshua, that You will send Your LIGHT to every Muslim to break in upon their darkness and to sweep away the dark deceit from their minds and hearts. I command the veil of lies over their minds and hearts to be removed and cast into the sea!

I pray in Your Name, Yeshua HaMashiakh (the Messiah), that all Muslims will repent in <u>sackcloth</u> (Kedar) and turn to You as their Savior and become <u>fragrance</u> in Your Kingdom. I pray they will <u>hear</u>, truly hear (<u>shma</u>) Your voice and truly <u>understand</u> Your Word. I pray they will stand in <u>silent</u> awe as they see Your <u>sign of the Cross</u> and will accept Your sacrifice for them and for their sins. I pray that the <u>burden</u> of their sins will be <u>carried</u> <u>away</u> by Your Blood. I pray they will see, truly see You and Your <u>Glory</u>. I pray they will be <u>encircled</u> by Your wings and by people who LOVE You and love them. I pray they will allow You to <u>enclose</u> them in Your arms. I pray You will <u>breathe</u> upon them the <u>breath</u> of the Ruakh HaKodesh (Holy Spirit)—that they will be filled with Your Ruakh (Spirit) and will become a mighty force in Your Kingdom that will <u>hasten</u> the day of Your Second Coming.

I command all the Muslim loudspeakers the whole world over to be <u>SILENCED</u> (Dumah)!! <u>BE</u> <u>SILENT</u> in YESHUA'S NAME, by the POW-

ER of Yeshua's BLOOD! All Muslim loudspeakers everywhere, malfunction! Be broken, never to be fixed. All hateful, evil Muslim teachings, <u>BE SILENCED</u>! All Muslim tapes, CDs, DVDs, videos, YouTube videos, all internet websites, etc., BE ERASED! All Muslim leaders, all anti-Yeshua, anti-Israel, anti-Christian, anti-God, anti-love, pro-violent, merciless theology, BE SILENCED FOREVER in the NAME of ALMIGTY GOD! All Muslim leaders, lose your voices! Islam, <u>be silenced</u> by an act of God that you cannot deny comes from GOD HIMSELF! AMEN! HALLELU-JAH!! I pray and beg You, Father God, Abba—Daddy, that it be an act by You that turns them to YOU!! Hallelujah! That turns them to Your Son, Yeshua (Issa) HaMashiakh.

O Yeshua Adonai, I pray the Muslims, after turning to You , will become <u>fruitful</u> (N'vayot) in Your Kingdom. I pray they will <u>germinate</u> and <u>flourish</u> and become a <u>prophetic</u> force against the enemy!

(Dumah: *undone utterly, cut down/off, fail, perish, cease*) Yes, Lord, I pray by the POWER of Your NAME that Islam be <u>undone utterly</u>. Islam, be <u>cut down</u> and <u>cut off</u>. Enemy—adversary—ha-satan behind Islam and behind everything against Israel and against God, <u>FAIL! CEASE! PERISH</u>! In the NAME of YESHUA! Be forever ceased. Be removed from the earth and cast into HELL FOREVER by the POWER of the BLOOD of YESHUA!

O Jesus, help us to pray all the prayers You need prayed for all the descendants of Yishma'el—and for all the Muslims today!

O Father, raise up the blacksmiths—engravers of precious metal! Mature them until they can do the work—the dangerous, difficult, <u>secret</u> work of "terrifying" and "casting out" "horns" and then of <u>crafting</u> beautiful artwork out of the Muslim culture and people. Empower the craftsman, Yeshua. Train them, equip them, prepare them, and propel them into this marvelous work.

13

PALESTINIANS–PHILISTINES–
HEBREW MEANING

On September 13, 2008 when Hurricane Ike hit Texas, I came across this verse.

> *Jer. 47:2-6 (NRSV) Thus says the LORD: See, waters are rising out of the north and shall become an overflowing torrent; they shall overflow the land and all that fills it, the city and those who live in it. People shall cry out, and all the inhabitants of the land shall wail. ... because of the day that is coming to destroy all the Philistines, to cut off ... every helper that remains. For the LORD is destroying the Philistines, the remnant of the coastland of Caphtor. Baldness has come upon Gaza, Ashkelon is silenced ... O remnant, ... How long until you are quiet? ... rest and be still.*

Today the Arabs in Israel call themselves Palestinians which comes from the word "Philistine." They never even wanted to call themselves this before 1967 because the word "Palestine" was used to refer to the land of Israel. The Romans are the ones who gave it that label. Well, when I read this verse, I was struck by the words, "*cut off ... every helper that remains.*" To me it is referring to every person or nation helping the Philistines who are warring against Israel! Well! America has been helping the Palestinians—especially in giving funds and weapons—against Israel! Thus an "overflowing torrent" (hurricane) has come again! This time in Texas (Hurricane Ike).

This caused me to look up the meaning of the word "Philistine." I was shocked by the meaning! It is H6430 פְּלִשְׁתִּי palishti which means "*inhabitant of the area.*" It is from H6429 פְּלֶשֶׁת paleshet which means "*rolling, i.e. migrating.*" How true that is for the Palestinians! "Paleshet" is from the root word H6428 פָּלַשׁ palash which means "*to roll (in dust): —roll (wallow) self.*"

At first I thought, "And they chose this name for themselves?!! Rolling and wallowing like pigs, yet they won't eat pork and consider pigs to be unclean?!!!" Then I began to pray.

O Lord, they ARE wallowing and rolling in dust and dirt. Telling their children to kill themselves and using women and children as shields and pawns in war is about as low as humans can go!!

O Lord Yeshua, open their eyes to see the filth they are wallowing in. Open their eyes to see!! Open every Muslim's eyes to see and be repulsed and to immediately stand up and leave the muck, and run to You to be cleansed of all the filth!!!

Then days later, as I studied further, I discovered that almost every time this word פָּלַשׁ "palash" was used in Scripture, it is referring to rolling yourself in the holy, purified ashes from the altar of repentance. So, it means the humility of "*Godly sorrow that leads to repentance*" (II Cor. 7:10) which brings eternal LIFE! I also remembered this verse. "*I will make an end of the pride of Philistia. I will take away its blood from its mouth and its abominations from between its teeth; it too shall be a remnant for our God; it shall be like a clan in Judah*" (Zech. 9:6-7) This brought me to my knees again.

So, Yeshua Adonai, may the Philistines—the Palestinians—come to the place of repentance—of rolling in the ashes of repentance; of turning to You, Yeshua, to be washed clean and to be grafted into the Olive Tree!! May they see the deceitful destruction of Islam, turn from it, and run to You, Lord. May they cry out in repentance to You. When Islam is destroyed, may they not mourn the loss long at all, but quickly turn to You in the Godly sorrow of repentance. May they soon find the JOY of being made pure in Your SALVATION!!! May they soon become a "remnant for You, like a clan in the tribe of Judah" in Your Kingdom!!!

47

14

GAZA–AZA–
AZAZ–PAZAZ

Then I felt led to look up the meaning of Gaza. It is H5804. It's really "Aza" עַזָּה. It means "*strong.*" It is from H5794 עַז Az which means "*strong, vehement, harsh: — fierce, greedy, mighty, power, rough, strong.*" The root word of this is H5810 עָזַז azaz, "*to be stout: —harden, impudent, prevail, strengthen (self), be strong.*"

O Adonai, may the Palestinians turn from being a <u>vehement, harsh, fierce, impudent, greedy, and hardened</u> to become <u>strong</u> in You. May they leave their religion of death, darkness, and destruction. May they repent in <u>ashes</u> and turn to You their Messiah, and find Living Water at Be'er-Sheva when they join Your people and make a covenant of Shalom in You, Yeshua, as the Philistine ancestor, Abimelech, made peace with Avraham and Yitz'khak. Then may they become a <u>strong</u>, powerful, mighty force in Your Kingdom—the Kingdom of Heaven. May they be <u>fierce</u> against the kingdom of darkness and <u>prevail</u> against the enemy, satan!!! Hallelujah, Amen!!

"Azaz" is the root word of "Philistine." If you put the Hebrew letter פ "p" in front of "azaz" you get "pazaz" H6338 פָּזַז. "*to refine (gold) — best (gold).*" "Paz" פָּז H6337 is "*fine, pure gold.*" The Hebrew letter פ "p" means "*mouth.*"

So, I began to pray this way. *Yeshua Adonai. May the Palestinians <u>hear</u> Your Word from Your <u>mouth</u> and may they receive it and be changed by it. Then may You give them a <u>mouth</u> to praise You and to speak Your powerful Word to others, that they may become <u>refined gold</u> in Your presence. May they become PAZ and PAZAZ!!*

15
AZAZEL–
SCAPEGOAT

Those words "Aza" and "Azaz" bring to mind another similar sounding word in Zechariah. Zechariah 14:4-6 speaks about an earthquake that will happen in the End Times when the Messiah returns and places His feet on the Mount of Olives. The eartquake will split the Mount of Olives from east to west creating a wide valley. Then it says, *"And you shall flee by the valley of the Lord's mountain, for the valley between the mountains shall reach to Azal.... Then the Lord my God will come, and all the holy ones with Him."*

That word "Azal" is used only 5 times in the Bible. The other four times it is referring to a man named Azal who had six sons, one named Yishma'el, of all things! This word "Azal" אָצֵל is H682 in the concordance, pronounced "Atzel." It means *"noble."* It has the letter צ in it which means *"hook"* in the middle of אֵל God. We are "noble" when we are "hooked" to the Lord! It comes from the root H680 אצל "atzal" that means *"to join"!* In Arabic the word "Azal" means *"eternity"* or *"morning of eternity"!* So we will flee to the "morning of eternity" where we will be "noble" and "joined" together as one—where Yishma'el and Yitz'khak will be joined together as one in Yeshua!

The direction of this escaping through this valley is the same direction the scapegoat on the Day of Atonement was sent. This word "Azal" also sounds similar to the Hebrew word for scapegoat, "azazel" "עֲזָאזֵל" (H5799). When you stop to think about the scapegoat, the story of Yitz'khak and Yishma'el fit very well! On the Day of Atonement, there are two goats brought to the Temple. The High Priest casts lots over them. One is chosen to be sacrificed on the altar at the Temple for sins. The other is chosen to be the scapegoat. All the sins of Israel are spoken as a confession over the scapegoat and then it is to be taken to the desert and abandoned there. You can read all about this in Leviticus 16:7-10, 15, 20-22.

Look at the similarities between those two goats and the two sons. God told Avraham to listen to his wife, Sarah, and to go ahead and send Yishma'el and his mother away. Later, God told Avraham to sacrifice Yitz'khak. (We know, of course, that in the end, God spared Yitz'khak.) When I ponder and meditate on this, a sense of inner awe begins to stir inside of me. It's the sense that there is something deeply profound here— that there is great, significant meaning in this for both the Jewish and the Arab people.

It is maybe too deep for us humans to grasp. But it is definitely true that all through history the Jewish people have suffered horrifically, while the Arab and Muslim people have mainly lived in desert regions of the world. It is also true that Yeshua, the Jewish Messiah, gave Himself as THE SACRIFICE for the sins of the whole world.

Here is a very interesting note about the practice of sending the scapegoat away. The High Priest always tied a red wool cord around the scapegoat's neck before they sent it away. It is recorded in Jewish history that one year the scapegoat returned several days later still wearing its red cord-collar. This shook the people up greatly because it was like their sins came back to haunt them.

What's interesting is that this is analogous to what is happening in history to Israel. The Arabs have returned from being banished by Avraham to irritate tiny Israel, just as the scapegoat returned, and just as Yishma'el apparently teased and irritated little Yitz'khak.

To finish the scapegoat story: at every Atonement Day since (after the goat came back that one time), the man who took the goat to the wilderness was told to lead it to a high precipice and throw it down to its death, so it couldn't possibly return. That solved their problem, but it was in direct disobedience to the command in Scripture which says to set the goat free in the wilderness (Lev. 16:22). It was apparently in God's plan to have the possibility of the scapegoat returning which I hope means, the descendants of Yishma'el will return in worship to the Lord!

16

LET THEM KNOW THE MOST HIGH GOD

Here's a prayer in Psalms partly for Ishmaelites that further supports this fact that God plans for the "scapegoat" to return. It doesn't sound too favorable until the end. Take special note of the last sentence.

Psalms 83 *O God, do not keep silent. Do not hold Your peace or be still, O God! ... those who hate You have raised their heads. They lay crafty plans against Your people. They consult together against those You protect. They say, "Come, let us wipe them out as a nation; let the name of Israel be remembered no more." They conspire with one accord; against You they make a covenant—the tents of Edom (Esau's descendants) ... Ishmaelites, Moab, ... Philistia, ... Assyria. ... who said, "Let us take the pastures of God for our own possession." ... Pursue them with Your tempest ... terrify them with Your hurricane. Fill their faces with shame, so that they may seek Your Name, O LORD* יהוה. *... Let them know that You alone whose Name is LORD* יהוה *are the MOST HIGH over all the earth.*

The Hebrew word for "Most High" is עליון Alyon (H5945). It means *"...supreme, ...most high"* The concordance says it comes from H5927 עלה alah which means *"to ascend, intrans. (be high) ..."*

The Hebrew word for God is H430 "Elohim" which comes from H410 אל El which means *"strength; mighty; espec. The Almighty: — God."* So I never connected Allah, the Muslim god, with the Hebrew word for God, since one starts with "e" and the other with "a." But this passage got me checking further, and I found that the Hebrew word H5920 עַל Al means *"the top; spec. the Highest (i.e. God) … Jehovah: —above, high, most High."* It also comes from the root word H5927 עָלָה alah! So, the name for the Muslim god could have come from a Hebrew name for the One, True God. Perhaps it is the name Yishma'el used and passed down! (The Arabic and Hebrew languages are very similar in pronunciation and meanings of words, eg., "Shalom" in Hebrew is "Selem" in Arabic and means the same thing.)

The sad thing is that even though the Muslims may be using a good name for their god, it is obviously not the Lord Most High. Mohammed's god is not the God of Avraham. We know this by the things radical Muslims do at the command of their god and their Koran. I'm referring to things like teaching their children to become suicide bombers, and sending them to mosques on Fridays at prayer time, or to weddings or birthday parties, or shopping centers, or funerals to blow people up. The Lord Most High—the God of Avraham—would not tell His people to do that. He did not allow Avraham to sacrifice his son. The prophets of the God of Avraham, Elijah and Elisha, raised children from the dead. They did not send them to their death. The God of Avraham sent His own Son to die to save all mankind, not to destroy them. He taught us to love our enemies and pray for them, not to hate or kill them. His Son told us to preach the Gospel to the whole world, to bring them into true LIFE not to death.

Another way to look at the word עָלָה "alah" is that their god wants to <u>ascend</u> to become <u>high</u>. If so, this would sound like the aspirations of the character in Isaiah 14:13-14 who used עָלָה "alah" in that exact way, and it would explain the propensity to the terror acts mentioned above.

But let's all pray earnestly and continually that the descendants of Yishma'el will come to know God "alone whose Name is Lord," who is the "Most High over all the earth," who loves each one of them and longs to bring them into His arms of LOVE, into ETERNAL LIFE!!! Actually He has planned this from the very beginning and has been "<u>paying attention</u>" to each one of them all through the ages, longing and waiting for the time for the fulfilling of His wonderful plan for them.

17

LIFT UP THE LORD IN ARAVAH

Here is another prophecy that hints to this wonderful plan. It is a very famous passage in Scripture. It is sung in Handel's "Messiah."

> Isaiah 40:3-5 (KJV) *The voice of him that crieth in the wilderness, Prepare ye the way of the LORD, make straight in the desert a highway for our God. Every valley shall be exalted, and every mountain and hill shall be made low: and the crooked shall be made straight, and the rough places plain: And the glory of the Lord shall be revealed, and all flesh shall see [it] together for the mouth of the LORD hath spoken [it].*

The Essenes at the time of Yeshua were trying to obey this verse which is why their society was set up in the desert at Qumran (where the Dead Sea Scrolls were discovered). They had separated themselves from their culture to live pure lives in order to "prepare … the way of the LORD … in the desert." Perhaps doing that did help in preparing the way for Yeshua to come. In studying the Dead Sea Scrolls, I learned that in their study of Scripture, the Essenes identified and made known all the signs of the coming Messiah. Their study most definitely had a huge role in helping the Jewish people recognize that Yeshua was the Messiah.

You might be wondering how in the world this could be speaking about God's plan for the Arabs. Well, let me explain. I was studying this passage in depth one day and was surprised by what I found. It was the meanings of the two different words translated as "wilderness" and as "desert" that really shook me.

The word translated as "wilderness" is the word used for "desert" in Hebrew today מדבר. No real surprise there except that the same letters with a tiny bit different pronunciation mean "speak." In the concordance it is H4057 which says it means "*a pasture*" or "*open field*" "*whither cattle are driven.*" The root word is H1696 דבר which, among its other meanings, besides "*to speak*" and "*to declare,*" has "*to subdue*" and "*to destroy*"*!!*

The word translated "desert" in the passage is H6160 ערבה pronounced "Aravah." It is the desert valley south of the Dead Sea (called the Salt Sea in Hebrew today). This valley, Arava, extends from the Salt Sea to the Red Sea. (It is also sometimes pronounced "Araba" because the Hebrew letter "B" can also be pronounced like a "V.") In the concordance it says, "*from H6150 (in the sense of sterility) a desert … sterile valley of the Jordan and its continuation to the Red Sea….*" The root word is H6150 ערב arav "*[rather identical with H6148 through the idea of covering with a texture]; to grow dusky at sundown —be darkened, (toward) evening.*" H6148 is the same letters ערב but pronounced "arab."

The Hebrew meanings of some other words in the passage are also very interesting. The word "prepare" is H6437 pana which means "*to turn; by impl. to face … —appear , at [-even] tide, behold, cast out … prepare … turn …*" At Blue Letter Bible, the concordance says, "*to turn … turn and do … show signs of turning, … turn back*"*!!* "Prepare" is only one meaning buried in all the other meanings of this word. "Turn" is its much more prominent meaning, it looks like to me. The word translated "way" is "derek." Besides "*way*" or "*road*" it also carries the implication of "*moral character.*" The word for "straight" can also mean "*to be right, … upright, … just.*" The word for "highway" is from the root word H5549 salel which means "*to lift up, cast up, … exalt, esteem highly.*"

Here's the Hebrew for verse three (read from right to left):

קול קורא במדבר פנו דרך יהוה ישרו בערבה
מסלה לאלהינו

Notice that there are no grammar marks in the Hebrew text. So, using

54

only these Hebrew words in the order they are written, with additional Hebrew meanings in brackets, and necessary grammatical words in paranthesis, and also putting the comma where the Jewish translators put it, here are the "bare bones" of this passage:

> Voice cries, proclaim in pasture [speak, subdue, destroy] turn (to the) way [moral character] (of the) LORD (be) straight [be right, just] and in Aravah [sterile valley, dusky, darkened] highway [exalt, lift up] our God (Elohenu).

To me, this looks like it could be telling us to:

Proclaim in the pasture (which I assume is the church), "Repent!" "Turn back to the Lord!" "Live a Godly life. Live right! Be just as God is just!" and "Subdue and destroy the enemy and his kingdom of darkness!!" In the sterile valley (the <u>dark</u>, <u>dusky</u> places of the world, the kingdom of <u>darkness</u>), lift up the Name of the Lord—lift up our God! Tell them about Yeshua!! Show them the way to the Lord!!"

With the Hebrew of the next verse actually including "will be's," "and's," and "the's," here are the "bare bones":

> Every deep valley [narrow gorge] will be lifted up and every mountain and hill [a place of illicit worship] will become low [humbled, humiliated], and the deceitful [sly, slippery] to level [uprightness] and the rough [bound up, impassable mountain chain] to plain [level valley].

This is so beautiful to me and it is so true. I've seen it happen in my own life and in the lives of many of my friends. Every <u>deep gulley</u> or <u>crack</u> or <u>deep</u> wound in our lives will be "lifted up" and healed. Every thing in our lives that lifts itself up against God—every bit of pride and idol worship—will be <u>humbled</u> and cleansed away. Our "deceitful," sinful, going-down-a-<u>slippery</u>-slope characters will be transformed to <u>uprightness</u> by Yeshua's blood and by the power of His Word. And the places in our hearts where we are <u>bound up</u>—the "rough," <u>impassable</u>, "mountains" in our lives that hold us back from God and block the Lord's Love from reaching the depths of our soul and setting us free—will be turned into beautiful, fertile <u>valleys</u>! The mountains will be "removed and cast into the sea" by the Power of Yeshua!

Since the root of that word "Aravah" is "arab" which sounds exactly like "Arab," maybe this is the Lord also telling us to lift up His Name and show the Way to Him in the Arab world!! Maybe it is emphasizing that all these things must also happen in the Arab world to the descendants of Yishma'el!!

THEN! The Jewish translators and the NRSV say "then" at the beginning of verse five. So, after we proclaim the Lord and show the Way to being truly healed and truly set free in the Lord, THEN the next verse will happen.

THEN the GLORY of the LORD יהוה shall be REVEALED,
and all flesh shall see [it] together for the mouth of the LORD
יהוה hath spoken!!!!

What a WONDERFUL, GLORIOUS day that will be!!!! And we will all see it together!!

So, I'm speculating from all this that perhaps, besides waiting for Israel to welcome Yeshua as their Messiah, the Lord is also waiting for the Arab world to find Him as their Savior and Healer before He returns! PERHAPS!

O Yeshua Adonai, I pray, please bring this Word of prophecy to complete fulfillment. Please help us to carry out Your commandment to lift up Your Name among the Arabs and the Muslims all over the world. Help us to teach them who You are. Help us to show them the way to Your Cross where their "deep" wounds can be healed; where the "rough places" in their hearts can be transformed into beautiful valleys—full of Your Love. Send Your workers to do this, Lord. Bring this to pass so that You can "reveal" your full "GLORY" to "all flesh" and we can all REJOICE "together"!

18

VALLEY
SACRED TO THE LORD

Here's another prophecy that hints even stronger to this plan of God. I put the Hebrew meanings of the words in brackets.

> Jer. 31:38-40 *The days are surely coming, says the LORD, when the city shall be rebuilt for the LORD from the tower of Hananel* [God has favored] *to the Corner Gate. And the measuring line shall go out farther, straight to the hill Gareb* [scabby, itchy], *and shall then turn to Goah* [loving]. *The whole valley of the dead bodies and the ashes* [H1880 *"ashes of sacrifice" "to anoint, to satisfy"*] [*"Philistine"* means *"to roll"* in ashes!] *and all the fields as far as the wadi Kidron* [H6939 *"dusky place"* from the root word H6937 qadar, the same root word that Yishma'el's second son's name, Kedar, is from!!], *to the corner of the Horse Gate toward the east, shall be sacred to the LORD. It shall never again be uprooted or overthrown.*

This valley is where the Muslims have a cemetery opposite the Jewish cemetery!! It IS a valley chock full of "dead bodies"!! Thousands of them!!! The Jewish people want to be buried there so they will be one of the first ones to rise again when the Messiah sets His feet on the Mount of Olives! The Muslims want to be buried there to desecrate the land so that same Messiah cannot enter the Temple by the East Gate (Golden Gate) as promised in Biblical prophecies. Using the Jewish, Biblical Law (Torah) against the Jewish Messiah—the Law that declares everyone must be purified before they enter the Temple—the Muslims are speculating that Yeshua won't be able to enter through that gate because He would be defiling Himself walking where dead bodies are buried!

So, here are the two sons of Avraham together in one place, in anticipation of the same Messianic event, albeit for opposing reasons! But, at least they are together! And it is in the place God says shall become SACRED to the LORD!!

I'm guessing also that the border described here going all the way to the hill Gareb probably includes the valley and hillside area south of the Temple called the City of David, which is now a huge, heavily populated, rather poverty stricken, Muslim neighborhood. But look at the promise hidden in the meanings of the words: favored of the Lord, from scabby and itchy to loving, and from repentance in "ashes" to being "sacred to the LORD"!! It sounds like a wonderful, fabulous plan to me!

Here's my prayer reaction when I first saw this. *O my word!! O my!! Praise the Lord. This is an unbelievably amazing prophecy, Lord! Amazing! Astounding! From being scabby and itchy—detestable (!) to LOVING in the "ashes" of sacrifice!! O Yeshua Adonai, You are going to turn that valley full of graves into a Holy, "Sacred" place for You!!! Amen! Let it be so! Bring it to pass! The valley of Yishma'el's son! The valley of both Jewish and Muslim graves!! You will bring the two together to make them Holy to YOU—holy ashes—holy, living sacrifices to You—anointed by You, that satisfy You!! Thank you, LORD, for Your awesome plan!*

How heavenly it will be!

It will be the fulfillment of what Yeshua said in John 10:16 (KJV).

Other sheep I have, which are not of this fold: them also I must bring, and they shall hear My voice; and there shall be one fold, and one shepherd.

19

GOD'S HEART IS TORN

I believe God's heart is torn as He sees Yishma'el's descendants suffering in the deceit of their false religion so far from the plan He has for them. I believe He mourns for them like He says here that He mourns for Moab.

> Jeremiah 48:30-31,36 *I Myself know his insolence, says the LORD; his boasts are false, his deeds are false. Therefore I wail for Moab; I cry out for all Moab.... My heart moans for Moab like a flute, and My heart moans like a flute for the people of Kir-heres....*

Moab is one of the two grandsons/sons of Lot. If God cares this much for the descendants of Avraham's nephew; if God weeps and moans for them, how much more does His heart pain and groan for the descendants of Avraham's own son?!!

Here is more Scriptural proof of the glorious plan God has for them. Look at this prophecy God spoke forth for them. They are going to praise God and be ministers; and God is going to accept their sacrifices on His altar, in HIS HOUSE!!!

> Isaiah 60:6-7 *A multitude of camels shall cover you, the young camels of* <u>Midian</u> *and Ephah; all those from* <u>Sheba</u> *shall come. They shall bring gold and frankincense, and shall proclaim the praise of the Lord. All the flocks of* <u>Kedar</u> *shall be gathered to you, the rams of* <u>Nebaioth</u> *shall minister to you; they shall be acceptable on My altar, and I will glorify My glorious house.*

> (Here's how CJB puts it.) *Caravans of camels will cover your land, ... bringing gold and frankincense, and proclaiming the praises of ADONAI. ... Kedar ... N'vaot ... They will come up and be received on My altar as I glorify My glorious house.*

If we are still not convinced, here is final, exciting Scriptural proof. God plans to "make Himself known" to the worshippers of Islam.

Isaiah 19:21-24 *On that day there will be an altar to the LORD* יהוה *in the center of the Land of Egypt, and a pillar to the LORD* יהוה *at its border. It will be a sign and a witness to the LORD of hosts in the land of Egypt; when they cry to the LORD because of oppressors, He will send them a Savior, and will defend and deliver them. The LORD will make Himself known to the Egyptians; and the Egyptians will know the LORD, and will worship.... On that day there will be a highway from Egypt to Assyria and the Assyrian will come into Egypt, and the Egyptian into Assyria and the Egyptians will worship with the Assyrians. On that day Israel will be the third with Egypt and Assyria, a blessing in the midst of the earth, whom the LORD of hosts has blessed, saying, "Blessed be Egypt My people, and Assyria the work of My hands, and Israel My heritage"*

Joel Chernoff, a leader of the Messianic Movement, said in a sermon given at a Messianic synagogue in Rochester, NY that the Biblical "Assyria" is Lebanon, Iraq and Syria. All three are neighbors of Israel and today they are all Muslim. Joel Chernoff pointed out that all these same nations along with all the countries that border Israel are missing in Ezekiel 38 where it lists the nations that will join together to fight in the final battle against Israel. So, since these bordering nations are not going to come against Israel, it goes without saying that they will be allies or friends of Israel, hopefully worshipping God with them as Assyria and Egypt in Isaiah 19 (above). This would include Jordan and Saudi Arabia!! This also means that Islam will definitely fall (at least in those countries)!!!

Hallelujah!!! Praise the Lord!! We thank you Lord Yeshua, Adonai that this is Your plan. We thank you that the oppression of Islam will be removed and that the descendants of Yishma'el WILL come to know You and worship You together with the descendants of Yitz'khak. Praise be to Your Name, Yeshua! May we soon see this day!!

20

TWO SONS, TWO GREAT NATIONS, TWO PLANS

Two great nations from two sons of Avraham: one chosen to be the greater; one the lesser—yet, both very important. Like the sun and the moon—two lights—two signs in the sky—two witnesses to God's Glory—one greater, one lesser, one to rule the day, the other the night (Gen. 1:14-16). I've been told by a Jewish person that Israel is often referred to as the sun. And I'm sure you're aware that Muslims display the crescent moon over all their mosques. God's meaning and significance for this, I cannot quite comprehend, but I know it is awesome because He is awesome!

Two sons. Both given special attention by God before birth and after. Both saved by the voice of God. Both alive through a miracle of God. Both born into a promised plan from God. Perhaps both figure into the End Time events. Perhaps not just one, but both are destined to hasten the Day of the Lord as they accept Yeshua and the two become the "one new man" in Him. Perhaps the "two witnesses" in Revelation will be one descendant from each of these two sons of Avraham, witnessing to the Glory and Power of God.

Lord, whatever Your End Time plan is for these two sons, we know it will be amazingly awesome and that Your Name will be Glorified. Bring it to pass soon, we pray.

In Yeshua's Name, Amen.

21

LET'S PRAY!

(ALL THE PRAYERS PUT TOGETHER)

O Yeshua, our Lord, help us to pray all the prayers You need prayed for all the descendants of Yishma'el—and for all the Muslims today!

O Adonai, You listened to Yishma'el's voice in the wilderness that day and paid attention. And I know You are still listening and paying attention to his descendants' cries of anguish and pain today. I know Your heart is torn by all their suffering. May they begin to cry out to You today so that You can answer them and save them from deception and oppression. May they be able to shma (hear) You, and shma (hear) Your Word. And may they drink from Your Be'er—Your Well of grace and salvation that makes us complete in You. May they find that Well-spring of Living Water that issues forth from Your Word—from the letters on Your tablet that make all things clear, distinct, and plain. May they turn to You, and drink from that Well until rivers begin to flow out of them, and they begin to declare Your Word to others. [Yishma'el's name (p. 26) Be'er Sheva (p. 14)]

Lord, we pray that what took place at Be'er-Sheva in the past will happen again. May both Yishma'el's and Yitz'khak's descendants come to know the Shalom that comes from meeting You and "calling on Your Name," and may they come to know the blessing of making an oath of shalom with their long lost brother! [Be'er Sheva (p. 13)]

O Adonai, Lord God of Heaven, I cry out for the demise of Islam in Yeshua's (Jesus') Name. By the Power of YESHUA'S (JESUS') BLOOD, I command Islam to come crashing down—"within the year"!! Within whatever year You have designated, Father. I command, by the POWER and AUTHORITY of the BLOOD of YESHUA for suicide bombings and terrorist attacks to come to an end—for all terrorism to cease. I command Jihad to come crashing down. Jihad, be annihilated. Power of Jihad be "crushed under our feet" and swept off the earth (Rom. 16:20; Ps. 18:42). Dark ages of Islam, be over! Be DONE!! I pray the LIGHT of God will come to all Muslims. I pray and beg You, Yeshua, send Your LIGHT to every Muslim to break in upon their darkness and to sweep away the dark deceit from their minds and hearts. I command the veil of lies over their minds and hearts to be removed and cast into the sea!

[Isaiah 21:16 (p. 34)]

Lord, I pray that the Islam religion, all factions and brands of it, be cast out. I pray the power of Jihad be cast out. I pray it be frightened away. May a terrifying fear come upon all in the Islamic religion, especially on the Jihadists, so terrifying that they will abandon Islam and will run to You, Yeshua; that they will cry out to You to be their Savior. I pray the Koran be frayed. I pray the power of the Koran come unraveled. I pray all the power of all the Muslim leaders, especially terrorist leaders and those against Israel, will come completely unraveled and be cast out.

In יֵשׁוּעַ Yeshua's Name—in You, our crucified and risen Redeemer's Holy Name, may all Muslims quake and tremble before You and bow in reverence and receive You as their Lord and Redeemer.

O Father, You have brought almost every kingdom to an end that has been against Israel. I pray in the Name of Yeshua—by Your un-surpassing Power, that Islam be brought to an end.

I speak in the Name of Yeshua, Islam religion, you come crashing down and be annihilated by the POWER of Yeshua's Name and by the POWER of Yeshua's shed BLOOD! [Zech. 1:20-21 (p.37)]

Almighty Father, may the dark ages of Islam be over. May all Muslims come to the LIGHT. May the veil be removed. May they repent in sackcloth (Kedar) and become fragrance (Mibsam and Bashemath) unto You, Lord. May they hear (shma) You, may they be silenced (Dumah) in awe of You. May they see Your sign, the Cross (Teman). May the burden (Massa) of their sins be carried away (also Massa). May they see Your Glory (Hadar). May they be encircled (Y'tur) by Your arms and enclosed (Y'tur) by Your wings, and breathed upon (Naphish) by Your Holy Ruakh, and may they hasten ("Kedmah") the Day of Your Coming!! [Sons' names (p. 28)]

I pray it again, Lord, in Your Holy Name, Yeshua HaMashiakh, that all Muslims will repent in sackcloth and turn to You, Yeshua, as their Savior and become fragrance in Your Kingdom. I pray they will hear, truly hear (shma) Your voice and truly understand Your Word. I pray they will stand in silent awe as they see Your sign of the Cross and will accept Your sacrifice for them and for their sins. I pray that the burden of their sins will be carried away by Your Blood. I pray they will see, truly see You and Your Glory. I pray they will be encircled by Your wings and by people who LOVE You and Love them. I pray they will allow You to enclose them in Your arms. I pray You will breathe upon them the breath of Your Holy Spirit—that they will be filled and refreshed with Your Ruakh and will become a mighty force in Your Kingdom that will hasten the day of Your Coming and that together with all Your other Believers, they will meet You in the air!

I command all the Muslim loudspeakers the whole world over to be SILENCED (Dumah)!! BE SILENT in YESHUA'S NAME, by the POWER of YESHUA'S BLOOD! All Muslim loudspeakers everywhere, malfunction forever! All hateful, evil Muslim teachings, BE SILENCED! All Muslim tapes, CDs, DVDs, videos, YouTube videos, all internet websites, etc., BE ERASED! All TV shows containing Islamic lies, be cancelled. All Muslim leaders, all anti-Yeshua, anti-Israel, anti-Christian, anti-God, anti-love, pro-violent, merciless theology, BE SILENCED FOREVER in the NAME of ALMIGTY GOD! All Muslim leaders, lose your voices! Islam, be silenced by an act of God that they cannot deny comes from GOD HIMSELF! AMEN! HALLALUJAH!! I pray and beg You, Father God, Abba—Daddy, that it be an act by You that turns them to YOU!! Hallelujah! That turns them to Your Son, Yeshua (Issa) HaMashiakh.

O Yeshua Adonai, I pray the Muslims, after turning to You, will become fruitful (N'vayot) in Your Kingdom. I pray they will germinate (N'vayot) and flourish (N'vayot) and become a prophetic (N'vayot) force against the enemy!

(Dumah: *brought to silence, undone, utterly, cut down, cut off, fail, perish, cease*) Yes, Lord, I pray by the POWER of Your NAME that Islam be undone utterly. Islam, be cut down and cut off. Enemy—adversary—hasatan behind Islam and behind everything against Israel and against God, FAIL! CEASE! PERISH! In the NAME of YESHUA! Be forever ceased. Be removed from the earth and cast into the LAKE OF FIRE FOREVER by the POWER of the BLOOD of YESHUA! [Sons' names (p. 28)]

[...*Let the desert and its towns lift up their voice, the villages that Kedar inhabits ... sing ... shout ... give glory to the LORD....* (Isaiah 42: 10-11) (p. 20)] Yes, Lord, please bring this to pass. May the descendants of Kedar, Yishma'el's son, which includes the Bedouins, come to know You and be so filled with the JOY of Your salvation that they will sing praises to you and will "shout" out their testimonies from the "mountain tops," giving You all the Glory! Amen! Hallelujah!!

O Yeshua, Adonai, I pray that out of Islam there will come a heap of testimonies—a monumental, magestic, memorial of testimonies of Your goodness; of You drawing all Muslims to Yourself! [(Gilead (p. 41)]

Lord Yeshua haMeshiakh, bring out the four quiet blacksmiths—engravers—designers—that will take the material of Islam and create something new and beautiful which will GLORIFY YOUR NAME!!!!

O Father, raise up these blacksmiths—the engravers of precious materal! Mature them until they can do the work—the dangerous, difficult, secret work of "striking down" and "casting out" the evil "horns" against You and of crafting beautiful artwork out of the Muslim culture and people. Empower the craftsman, Yeshua. Train them, equip them, prepare them, and propel them into this marvelous work. [Blacksmiths (p. 43)]

[Palestinian: Palash: *to roll (in dust): —roll (wallow) self*) (p. 46)] O Lord, they ARE <u>wallowing</u> and <u>rolling in dust</u> and dirt. O Lord Yeshua, open their eyes to see the filth they are wallowing in. Open their eyes to see!! Open every Palestinian's eyes to see and be repulsed and to immediately stand up and leave the muck, and run to You to be cleansed of all the filth!!! May they come to the place of repentance—of rolling in the <u>pure ashes</u> of repentance—of turning to You, Yeshua, to be made holy and to be grafted into the Olive Tree!! May all Muslims see the deceitful, destruction of Islam, and turn from it and run to You, Lord. May they cry out in repentance to You. When Islam is destroyed, may they not mourn the loss, but quickly turn to You in Godly sorrow of repentance. May they soon find the JOY of being made pure in Your SALVATION!!! May they soon become a "*remnant for You, like a clan in the tribe of Judah*" in Your Kingdom!!!

O Adonai, may the Palestinians turn from being a "<u>*vehement, harsh, fierce, impudent, greedy, and hardened*</u>" (Aza p. 48) people to becoming <u>strong</u> (also Aza) in You. May they leave their religion of death, darkness, and destruction. May they repent in <u>ashes</u> and turn to You, their Messiah, and find Living Water at Be'er-Sheva when they <u>join</u> Your people and make a covenant of Shalom in You, Yeshua. May they do as the Philistine ancestor, Abimelech, who made peace with Avraham and Yitz'khak. Then may they become a <u>strong</u>, powerful, mighty force in Your Kingdom—the Kingdom of Heaven. May they be <u>fierce</u> (also Aza) against the kingdom of darkness and <u>prevail</u> against the enemy, ha-satan!!! Hallelujah, Amen!!

O Yeshua Adonai, may the Palestinians hear Your Word from Your mouth (פ pey) and may they receive it and be changed by it. Then may

You give them a <u>mouth</u> to praise You and to speak Your powerful Word to others, that they may become <u>refined gold</u> in Your presence. May they change from being Az to Paz (fine, pure gold) and from Azaz to become PAZAZ (refined, best gold)!! [Gaza—Aza—Azaz —Pazaz (p. 48)]

O Praise the Lord! Bring us, Lord, from being <u>scabby and itchy</u> and detestable to <u>LOVING</u> in the <u>ashes of sacrifice</u>!! Thank you that this is exactly what You do for us! Hallelujah!! Thank you for Your Love and Sacrifice that accomplish this for us. Do it for all the Muslims, for all the descendants of Yishma'el and for all the descendants of Yitz'khak!! Thank you, Yeshua! [Jer. 31:38-40 (p. 57)]

O Yeshua Adonai, I pray, please help us to carry out Your commandment to <u>lift up Your Name</u> among the Arabs and the Muslims all over the world. Help us to teach them who You are. Help us to show them the way to Your Cross where their <u>deep</u> wounds can be healed; where the "rough places" in their hearts can be transformed into <u>beautiful valleys</u> full of Your Love. Send Your workers to do this, Lord. Bring this to pass so that You can "reveal your full GLORY" to "all flesh" and we can all REJOICE "together"! [Isaiah 40:3-5, (p. 53)]

O Yeshua Adonai, You are going to do this amazing, astounding thing! You are going to turn Kidron valley, full of tombs, into a Holy, "Sacred" place for You!!! Amen! Bring it to pass! The valley of Yishma'el's son, Kedar! The valley of both Jewish and Muslim graves!! You will bring them together as "one flock" with "One Shepherd." You will make them Holy to YOU— holy "ashes"—holy, living sacrifices to You—<u>anointed</u> by You, that <u>satisfy</u> You!! HALLELUJAH! Thank you, LORD, for Your awesome plan! Bring it to pass soon, Lord. Please cause it to begin to happen! Let us see this glorious thing begin to take place!!! [Jer. 31:38-40 & John 10:16 (p. 57)]

[Ishmaelites ... that they may seek Your Name, O LORD יהוה. Let them know that You alone whose Name is LORD יהוה are the MOST

HIGH over all the earth. (Psalms 83) (p. 51)] Abba Father we pray earnestly and continually that Yishma'el's descendants will come to know You! You "alone whose Name is Lord" the "Most High over all the earth," the God who loves each one of them and longs to bring them into Your arms of LOVE, into ETERNAL LIFE!!! You have planned this from the very beginning. You have been "paying attention" to each one of them all through the ages, longing and waiting for the time for the fulfilling of Your wonderful plan. Bring it to pass soon, Lord. Bring them to Yourself soon!

O Father in heaven, may that <u>heap of testimonies</u> (Gilead) from Yitz'khak and Yishma'el's descendants, and from all the nations grow higher and higher!! O Father, this is Your will!! O Lord, please gather us all in to that <u>heap of testimonies</u> of <u>hearts made white</u> (Lebanon). Bring us all in until there is no more room—no empty place in Your vast, infinite heaven; until there are no more souls to bring in, including Muslim souls; and, Lord, until there is no one left out, including Muslim, Jewish, and Gentile people! Yes, Lord, bring this to pass. Let it be fulfilled soon! Please, Lord, please soon let us begin to enjoy the <u>heap of testimonies</u> from all those down through the ages whose <u>hearts are made white</u> by Yeshua's Blood. [Gilead and Lebanon (p. 41)]

O Yeshua our Messiah, bring us to the day when Your plan will be fulfilled when Yishma'el will no longer be the world's scapegoat, and Yitz'khak will no more be treated like a lamb for the world's slaughter-house. Bring us to the day when all their descendants will accept Your suffering that fulfilled both those sacrifices. Bring us to the day when You will return and will "split the Mt. of Olives," and we, Your Believers, will all "escape through the valley to Azal," the <u>morning of Eternity</u>. Bring us to that day when we will all be <u>noble</u> and righteous by the cleansing of Your Blood and will all, including all the believing descendants of Yitz'khak and Yishma'el, be <u>joined</u> as one in You, Yeshua. [Azazel (Zech. 14:4-6) (p. 49)]

O Lord God of Heaven above, we praise You as we pray for the day when all the nations surrounding Israel will worship You together with Israel!! In Your HOUSE!!! As You promised in Your Word!! Hallelujah!! Amen!! Bring it to pass!! [Isaiah 60:6-7 and 19:21-24 (p. 59-60)]

O Lord Most High, our Heavenly Father-Abba-Daddy, We wait in glorious, excited expectation for that day when Your End Time plan for the elder son of Avraham will be fulfilled, whatever it is. Praise Your Name!! We know it will be awesome because You are ASTOUNDINGLY AWESOME!! And we know that Your Name will be Glorified through it all because You are GLORIOUS!! Bring Your FULL plan for Yishma'el to pass soon, please, we pray.

And, Father, we want to end by praying again with Avraham, believing that You are answering us: if only Yishma'el's descendants could also come to believe and live forever in Your presence with all Your other Believers!

[Gen. 17:20 (p. 11)]

In Yeshua's All-Powerful, Holy Name we pray all these prayers, Amen.

This book is available at
olivepresspublisher.org
amazon.com
barnesandnobles.com
and more.

www.ingramcontent.com/pod-product-compliance
Lightning Source LLC
Chambersburg PA
CBHW060147050426
42448CB00010B/2336